Laughter 'N Blues

Humorous Stories from the Nashville, Tennessee Police Department

Written by

Bobby J. Bass, Retired

Nashville P. D.

Table of Contents

INTRODUCTION 3
DEDICATION 4
CHAPTER I 7
CHAPTER II 17
CHAPTER III 31
CHAPTER IV 49
CHAPTER V 63
CHAPTER VI 83
CHAPTER VII 97
CHAPTER VIII 117
CHAPTER IX 133
CHAPTER X 139

Introduction

When reflecting back on my 25 years as a police officer, many realizations come to mind. Foremost is the fact that in those 25 years, I experienced almost every emotion known to man – love, hate, fear, etc. However, the emotion that was my ally, the emotion that helped me survive, was HUMOR. Not to say that the violence observed is not etched in my mind, it is, but the humor somewhat diminishes the unpleasant memories.

The events depicted in this book are true, only the names have been changed to protect …….. Me.

Dedication

It has been said that it takes a special person to be the spouse of a police officer. My wife, Virginia, gives substance to this saying. She stuck by me and held our marriage together for seventeen years of my twenty-five year career. Yes, Virginia, there is a life after the Police Department.

"The test of a first-rate intelligence is the ability to hold two opposed ideas in mind at the same time and still retain the ability to function."

- F. Scott Fitzgerald

All Rights Reserved © 2010 Bobby J. Bass

Disclaimer and Terms of Use: No information contained in this book should be considered as physical, health related, financial, tax, or legal advice. Your reliance upon information and content obtained by you at or through this publication is solely at your own risk. The author assumes no liability or responsibly for damage or injury to you, other persons, or property arising from any use of any product, information, idea, or instruction contained in the content provided to you through this book.

Chapter I

This Is Where It All Started

That's me 2nd from the right taking the oath

It was 1961 and I was being sworn in as a police officer on the Nashville Police Department. The oath that I was repeating was serious enough; "protect life and property." The times were serious also. JFK was president. He had initiated the Bay of Pigs invasion. It, of course, had failed. The minimum wage was $1.15 an hour. Police officer pay would start at $318.00 per month which equated to $1.83 per hour. Not bad for a high school graduate, I thought.

Our country was in the middle of the civil rights movement. That movement apparently had not progressed to the police department.

At the first roll call I attended, the black officers were required to fall in to the rear. They were not allowed back then to answer calls involving white complainants.

I soon learned we were brothers regardless of society's view. We fought together and we laughed together, the laughter came first. Also back then, there were no female officers in the field.

Our roll call was held in a small assembly room adjacent to the city court room. After roll call, we went down the stairs to the "ramp" where the previous shift lined up the patrol cars.

We were required to be at roll call on the half hour, roll call began 15 minutes later. On the half hour, the desk sergeant would call the assembly room and give the names of the officers who would be assigned inside that shift. It was called, affectionately, "the shit detail."

The practical jokes would start immediately. My name was called out on the third day. With nervous anticipation, I reported to the desk sergeant. There I was greeted, if you could call it that, by Sergeant Morris. He was a gray headed man in his late 60's, with a very gruff voice.

Sergeant Morris smoked Salem cigarettes, which he kept in his back pocket and, naturally, when he sat, mashed the cigarettes flat. Later, after I felt comfortable conversing with him, I bummed a cigarette from him. I made note that the cigarette was flat. That was a mistake. "If you don't want that fucking cigarette, give it back. You bum a cigarette and then criticize it for being flat? Go buy you own fucking cigarettes."

Anyway, it was my third day and I was getting my assignment from Sergeant Morris. Directly behind his desk, was the switchboard. This would be my assignment for the night. I was given brief instructions and told to do the best I could. After about 30 minutes, I received a call and the voice on the other end said, "This is the phone company and we're conducting a test. Please stand back 10 feet from the console and whistle." Being young and naïve, I did so. Sergeant Morris turned in his chair and smiling, said, "We're getting them young and stupid." I sensed that I had been had.

While working on the switchboard, I had an incoming call. The board was covered with calls in and a lot going out so I answered one call quickly. We were supposed to answer by "Police Department, Officer (name)." I answered, "Officer Bass." Then the caller said, "Officer who?" I was getting very irritated by then, so I answered, "Officer Bass, damn it, B-A-S-S."

Then I heard a frightening sound from the caller. He said, "Well, Officer Bass, this is the Mayor, M-A-Y-O-R, connect me with the Chief." I said, "Yes sir, right away." I connected him to the Chief's office and in about five minutes, the Chief walked in to Sergeant Morris' office and asked, "Who do you have on the switchboard, Sergeant?" Sergeant Morris answered, "I got a new man on it Chief and he's doing the best he can."

The Chief said, "O.K. Sergeant." He left and went back to his office. I said to myself, "thank you, Sergeant Morris."

Another assignment on the "shit detail" was the radio room. A few weeks after the switchboard duty, I got the dreaded call from Sergeant Morris. I went to his office and he said, "Go to the radio room. You'll be a complaint clerk – it's down the hall and up the stairs." The radio room was located next to Central Records. There was a dispatcher and four complaint clerks.

The complaint clerk's job was to answer the phone, get all the pertinent information from the caller, fill out a card and send it, by means of a conveyer, to the dispatcher.

As a complaint clerk, I remember one night in particular. The radio had been exceptionally quiet when a calm voice from one of the cars came over the air. It was Officer John Harris. Officer Harris, like me, had been an officer for just a few weeks.

"Car 8 to headquarters, we're following a 60 Chevy on Buchanan Street going west. Car 8, he's doing about 70. Car 8, the son-of-a-bitch is running." Everyone in the radio room was cracking up. The dispatcher radioed Harris. "Car 8, repeat." There was a moment of silence, then, "Car 8, signal 9 (disregard) we got him."

One of the older officers in the radio room related an incident that occurred a few years prior to my becoming an officer. He told that the chief then was Chief Hogan.

Well, Chief Hogan had taken a trip to Los Angeles, California by means of his police vehicle. One night a transmission came over the air and the voice said, "Car 101 to headquarters." Car 101 was no other than Chief Hogan.

The dispatcher said, "Go ahead, chief." "How do you read me?" "Loud and clear, chief." "I'm going over the Golden Gate Bridge at this time."

There were a few seconds of silence and then a soft voice from one of the cars in the field, "Jump you son-of-a-bitch." I was told that Chief Hogan offered everything but his life for the identity of that voice. He never found out who it was.

Another transmission which struck me as humorous was made by Officer Raymond Burton. Officer Burton was a big, black officer, who at first glance, was very intimidating. In reality, he was a nice, gentle guy. One night, Officer Burton's voice came over the radio. "Car 2, give me a record check on the following subject." At this point, Burton gave the subject's name, age, and date of birth. There was a short pause and then, "Get off my fucking foot, boy."

A few months later, the radio room was moved to the lobby. It was enclosed by glass and therefore became known as the "cage." In retrospect it wasn't planned professionally.

A person could stand in the lobby and by merely looking into the radio room, be able to gather information as to which cars were out of service and what parts of the city were left unprotected.

The Lieutenant's office was directly behind the radio room. That is where good ole Sergeant Morris was stationed. By the way, Sergeant Morris had been promoted and was now Lieutenant Morris.

One night, I was assigned as dispatcher. One of the complaint clerks that night was Officer Ron Batts. Batts had a talent for impersonating people and had the voice of Lieutenant Morris down to perfection. Working in the booking room, was Officer Don Warren.

Warren was a somewhat nervous person who had an enormous desire to please his superiors. Officer Warren had been in my rookie class.

I recall an incident that, at the time wasn't funny at all, but afterwards seemed hilarious.

Our rookie class was on the gun range and Warren was firing the Thompson sub-machine gun, when he did the inexcusable.

During firing, for some unknown reason, he let go of the gun with one hand while continuing to fire. Well, the barrel of the gun went straight up shooting off his ball cap.

Chapter II

The Booking Room and Traffic Division

Officer Batts and I concocted up this joke to play on Warren. Batts got on the phone and called the booking room. In his Lieutenant Morris voice, he said, "Warren, come down to my office." "Yes sir, Lieutenant." In about 30 seconds (the booking room was on the third floor and we were on the first floor) Warren walked in the Lieutenant's office. "Yes sir, Lieutenant." We of course were watching with great anticipation. As I mentioned, the radio room was enclosed by glass and we had an unobstructed view of the action. "I didn't call you, Warren. Get your ass back upstairs." Officer Warren left with a somewhat puzzled look on his face.

After about five minutes, Batts got on the phone again. "I thought I told you to come by my office, Warren." "I did Lieutenant." "Are you calling me a liar, Warren?" "No sir, Lieutenant." "Then get your ass down here." This time, in about 20 seconds, Warren showed up at the Lieutenant's door. "Yes sir, Lieutenant, You called." "Warren this is the last time I'm gonna tell you, get your ass back up to the booking room. This time we waited about ten minutes. "Warren, are you gonna come to my office or not?" "I did, Lieutenant, and you said you didn't call me." "Warren, this is the last time I'm gonna tell you. "Get your ass down here or I'm gonna suspend you." Well you can imagine what happened when Warren showed up at the Lieutenant's door the third time. We were rolling. After the Lieutenant screamed at Warren for about five minutes he picked up the phone and called me. "Bass, call car 1 (downtown car) and tell them to come get Warren and take him to General Hospital. The mother-fucker's gone crazy." We then had to let the Lieutenant in on our joke. He only screamed at us for about two minutes. I always suspected, though, that he got a kick out of the joke.

In April 1963, the citizens of Nashville voted to adopt the Metropolitan Government concept. The city of Nashville would encompass the entire county. The various divisions of the Police Department would be expanded. I requested and was granted, a transfer to the traffic division. I would start out riding a 3-wheel motorcycle, working mainly traffic control. Remember Officer Burton, the black officer who had inadvertently transmitted the request for the suspect to get off his foot? Well, Officer Burton also was assigned to a 3-wheel in the predominantly black section of town.

One day, I happened to be in his area working a wreck when a young man about 12 years old, walked up to me and said, "Do you know Officer Burton?" "Sure, I know him, why?" "He's scared of that motorcycle." "Why do you say that?" "Cause he won't ride it on the street. He rides it on the sidewalk." Later, when I ribbed Officer Burton about what the young man said, he, of course, denied it.

Let me introduce you to an Officer named Bobby Lewis. Bobby was much of a man; he stood about 6'7" and weighed about 275 pounds. Bobby was an easy going guy with a great personality. Someone once asked him if he had a lot of guys resist arrest. He said he very rarely had to charge and one with resisting arrest. Wonder why?

One evening, he was the backup office on a call where a man was threatening to jump from the fifth floor of a downtown hotel. When Bobby arrived on the scene, the guy was standing on a ledge outside the window five stories up.

There was a crowd gathered, including officers, watching from the ground level. Bobby asked permission to go up to the fifth floor to talk to the guy. The Sergeant gave him permission and Bobby proceeded to take the elevator up to the fifth floor.

He found the room where the guy was threatening to jump. Bobby entered the room and went to the window. When seeing Bobby approach, the guy said, "don't come any closer or I'll jump." Bobby calmly said, "Ok, Buddy, you have a choice to make. You can either jump or come back in the window. I'm going to count to ten and if you don't come back in or jump, I'm gonna push your ass off the ledge and you're gonna bust it on the ground."

The guy apparently believed Bobby because he quickly came back in the window. I think, maybe, Bobby's size had something to do with his decision.

One time Bobby got sued, along with two other officers, for police brutality. The guy who brought suit claimed that Bobby hit him after he got out of the police car at headquarters.

When it went to trial, the man was represented by an attorney who had a reputation for bringing suit against police officers. He lost almost all of the cases. Anyway, during the trial, the man got on the stand and said that he had been arrested and when he arrived at headquarters, Bobby got him out of the car and when he asked a question; Bobby hit him in the head. He stated that the two other officers did nothing to stop Bobby from hitting him.

When Bobby took the stand to testify in his defense, he asked the Judge if he could approach the plaintiff who was sitting at a table with his attorney. The Judge gave Bobby permission to approach. Then Bobby said, "I did not strike this man and I would like to show you why I did not." Bobby then asked the man to rise and when he did, Bobby, remember now he was 6'7" and 275, put his arms around the man, chest high and lifted him off the floor. The man's feet were dangling and he was helpless. Bobby then said, "You see Judge, I didn't have to hit this man to control him, I could easily control him this way." The Judge told Bobby to put the man down and he did. Of course, the man's attorney was very upset with Bobby's display. The man lost the case and Bobby was found "not guilty" of police brutality.

One of the not so pleasant duties encountered in patrol was to take persons, who were considered mentally unstable by city physicians, to a mental institution in the city.

One night, about 3 a.m., we received a call to go to the city hospital and transport a man to the mental facility. We picked him up and transported him to be evaluated by doctors at the mental institution.

On arrival, we were waiting in the examining room for the doctor. They had to notify the doctor on call and in about 45 minutes, he came to the exam room. You could tell that he was irritated for having to get out of bed in the middle of the night.

He sat at his desk and began asking the man for pertinent information. When he got to the part about "family history", and after answering questions about mother, father, grandparents, etc., he asked the man if he had any brothers or sisters. The man, now also irritated, said, "Yeah, I've got seven brothers and six sisters, why?"

The doctor, in an aggravated tone, said, "If you get sick while you're here, we need to know who to call." The man replied, "Hell doctor, my brothers or sisters can't do a damn thing if I'm sick." The doctor threw down the man's chart and said, "Take him to a room, I'm through with him." We were trying hard not to laugh out loud, but we did as soon as the doctor left the room.

It was the early 60's and I was in my mid-twenties. Some would say that I had a "baby face." So, one day Sergeant Morris called me into his office and said he had a special assignment for me and another officer.

The other officer was Jim Jefferson, a young guy who came on the force with me. Sergeant Morris briefed us and said that the "gay" problem had increased in the city and he wanted us to catch some of them attempting to solicit young guys.

We were to go into restrooms and if a man approached us and attempted to engage in a homosexual act with us, we were to arrest that person. All the gay guy had to do was touch our private parts and that constituted a violation of the law called "public lewdness."

Well one day, we were working a downtown parking lot that had a well-known reputation for gays hanging out and soliciting young potential partners in the restroom. There was a waiting area where they would sit and size up their prey. Jim and I went into the waiting area separately and sat there.

Jim went into the restroom and immediately a man got up and followed. In a couple of minutes, Jim came out and sat back down. The man came out and also took a seat. I was watching all of the "action" from my vantage point. So Jim went back into the restroom and, again, the man followed him. In about five minutes, Jim came back and the man followed again.

Then, Jim went into the restroom a third time and the man followed again. Well, in about two minutes Jim and the man came back out and Jim motioned for me to follow him out of the waiting area. We went back to our car and I asked him what happened in the restroom. He said that the first two times, the guy just looked at him but made no move. He said when he went in the third time, the guy, again, looked at him and smiled. Jim said that it dawned on him what was happening so he looked at the guy and said," apparently, you think I'm gay and I think you are gay so I'll set you straight. I'm a cop trying to catch gay guys and furthermore. I'm working this restroom so you can get your ass out of here so I can do what I came here to do, catch gays. You understand?" He said the guy said, "Yes sir, I'll leave." And he did.

Officer Jefferson and I had a call that produced some laughs one night. There was a pancake restaurant near the Vanderbilt University campus and was frequented by the college students. On this particular night, we received a call of a male that had exposed his privates to a couple of the females who were dining at the restaurant.

On arrival, we were met by two young ladies who said that a male had walked up t the "full view" window beside their table and pulled out his penis and exposed himself.

We asked for a description by asking the following questions; "was he white or black?" Neither lady knew the answer. "How old was he?" Again, neither none knew. "O.K., How tall was he?' They didn't know. "How much did he weigh?" They had no answer. "What kind of clothes was he wearing?" They could not tell us.

So, all we had, was, a penis they had viewed through the window. Needless to say, we didn't ask any more questions because the last one we would have asked was, "Do you think you could identify this subject if you saw him again?"

We held back our laughter until we got back into the patrol car.

Working in the traffic division resulted in appearing in traffic court frequently. On one appearance day, there happened to be a speeding case called before my cases. The ticket had been issued by Officer Richard Lane. Lane was a very distinguished looking black officer. He was gray headed, tall and spoke very eloquently. I was therefore surprised, when the defendant stated, "Judge I might have been speeding but when Officer Lane gave me the ticket, he called me a mother-fucker." "Officer Lane" the judge inquired, "Is this true?" "I might have your honor, but he pissed me off." "Case dismissed. I'll see you in my chambers, Officer Lane." I don't know what went on in the judge's chambers but Officer Lane was on duty the next day and as I passed him in the hall, he looked at me and just smiled.

In October 1963, several traffic officers were promoted to sergeant. Some of the promotions were "solo" (two wheel) motorcycle officers. These officers left their vacated motorcycles at headquarters. In an effort to keep the solos running and the maintenance up to date, the motorcycles were assigned to the 3-wheel officers to ride to and from work. Officer Calvin Bennett was assigned one such motorcycle. As you probably know, or can imagine, there is a lot of difference in riding a 3-wheel as opposed to a solo motorcycle.

Bennett, I might add, was an almost exact clone of Lieutenant Morris. He had a very gruff voice and probably never heard of Amy Vanderbilt.

The first day Bennett was assigned the solo; he called the office and informed the traffic sergeant that he didn't want the solo. The sergeant told him to just bring it to headquarters and turn it in. Bennett informed the sergeant, "If you want this mother-fucker, you can come and get it. I liked to got killed three different times just getting this mother-fucker to my house. I'm not about to strap my ass on it again." The motorcycle was picked up at Officer Bennett's house the next day.

Chapter III

Motorcycles and the Raiders

These are the infamous "Raiders"

It's 1964. The surgeon general cites the health hazards of cigarette smoking. Miniskirts are introduced that year. In March, a motorcycle enforcement squad was formed. The squad consisted of ten motorcycle officers under the leadership of Sergeant Kerry Norman. I was fortunate to be selected as one of the ten. We could be called "the Raiders". Our job was selective enforcement of the traffic laws. We would work nights and we would work the so called dangerous streets of the county. The squad would focus primarily on DUIs, reckless driving and speeding. After just a few months, I realized I had never really been hot or cold before. Now I knew what it felt like to survive the elements. In any event, these times would expand my sense of humor.

Let me introduce you to Officer Marty Crandall. Officer Crandall, in his youth, was a newspaper delivery boy. He had carried heavy bags of papers which resulted in his slow, shuffling walk as an adult. He was a fanatic about keeping his vehicle, whatever it might be, in spotless condition. He had a dry sense of humor, much like that of Yogi Berra.

I remember one time when Crandall was testifying in court concerning a stop sign ticket he had issued. The defendant had an attorney representing him. "Officer Crandall, you say that you observed my client run a stop sign?" "Yes sir." "And what time of day was it?" "9:15 pm." "And where were you positioned when you observed my client run the stop sign?" "About a half block away." "Was it daylight or dark?" "It was dark." "Let me see if I understand your testimony Officer Crandall. You were a half block away from the stop sign, in the dark, and you observed my client run the stop sign." "Yes sir, I did." The attorney turned to the courtroom audience and gave a pompous smile, "Just how far can you see at night, Officer Crandall?" "Well, I can see the moon and it's 300,000 miles away." The entire court erupted in laughter. Even the judge was laughing. The only ones who were not laughing were the attorney and the defendant.

I mentioned before the 3-wheel assignment. Well, Officer Crandall began his traffic career as I had, riding a 3-wheel and working traffic control. One morning Marty was assigned to a traffic light at the foot of one of the bridges that emptied traffic into the downtown area. This particular light had a long cord which allowed the officer to work the light by hand. The officer working the light could keep the signal green at longer intervals thus allowing the traffic to flow freely. We had a lieutenant who routinely drove around the city checking the rush hour traffic. On the morning that Officer Crandall was working the light in question, the lieutenant came on the air, "204 to headquarters. Do you have anyone working the light at Fourth and McGavock?" "10-4, 204. 235 is assigned there." "204, the traffic on the bridge is backed up for miles and not moving." "Headquarters to 235." There is a muffled reply. "235, go ahead." "Are you at Fourth and McGavock?" "10-4." "204, I'll go by and see what the problem is."

After fighting his way through the traffic and finally across the bridge, the lieutenant pulled up to the corner. He could see the 3-wheel but no officer in sight. He noticed the cord from the signal light and traced it to the back of the 3-wheel. For those of you not familiar with 3-wheel motorcycles, the back part is a compartment approximately 4' by 5'. It is used for storage of reports, rain gear, supplies, etc. Well, as the lieutenant examined the situation more closely, he discovered that the cord went inside the back compartment of the 3-wheel. He opened the lid and there, inside, was Crandall. You see, it was a cold morning and he had gotten inside to keep warm. Crandall told me later that when the lieutenant got out of his car, he didn't even open the door; he came out through the vent glass. Needless to say, Crandall didn't work that light for a long time after that morning.

Now, Crandall and I were two of the "Raiders". One summer night there was a demonstration in the downtown area. People were marching for a cause and we were sent to one of the outlying areas to stand by. As I mentioned, Sergeant Norman was our supervisor and we decided to get one on Marty. When we rode as a squad, we rode a formation of twos with the sergeant leading and when we parked the motorcycles, we lined them up accordingly. Sergeant Norton walked off to the side, away from the motorcycles, and engaged Crandall in conversation. While Marty's attention was diverted, we took his motorcycle and rolled it around the block, out of sight. When Sergeant Norton and Crandall walked back toward the motorcycles, I, excitedly, told the sergeant, "The captain's calling you sarge." Sergeant Norton picked up his mike and said, "10-4 captain, we're on our way. They need us now, men. Let's go." We all jumped on our motorcycles, that is, all but Crandall. He didn't have one on which to jump. We sped off in formation and went around the block. We all cut the engines and coasted to a stop. Then, we got off our motors and walked to the corner where we could peer around the building and see Crandall. He was standing there where his motorcycle had been parked, and as he always did when he was confused, scratching his genitals. We got back on our motors and rode back to him. Sergeant Norton got off his motorcycle and walked up to him. "Why didn't you come with us when I gave the order, Crandall?" "I ain't got no motorcycle, sarge." "Where the hell is it?" "I don't know where it is sarge, but I know where it ain't. It ain't here."

The next night, an opportunity arose which gave me a chance to pull one on Crandall again. As I mentioned, we had been sent to this outlying area to stand by in case there were problems with the demonstrators. We were in a business district which consisted of a furniture store, transmission shop and a dairy dip. There really wasn't much activity going on which resulted in our somewhat boredom. I happened to be standing on the sidewalk, sort of away from the rest of the guys. This big, black Buick stopped and there were two young ladies inside. They asked for directions but I could see that they had local tags. The passenger was an average looking girl about 25. The driver was about the same age but had an outstanding feature. She was big, and I do mean big. After a minute or so of conversation, I asked the ladies to pull to the end of the block where it was dark. They did so, willingly. Then I walked over to Marty and said, "See that car parked at the end of the block?" "Yeah, I see it." "Well, there are two airlines stewardesses in that car and I think they want to play." "Well let's go" he said. We walked to the car and the girls had separated. The passenger was in the backseat. The big girl was still under the wheel. I, of course, told Crandall to get up front. It was very dark and he could not see inside the vehicle very well. He opened the front door and got inside. I got in the back. Crandall took off his helmet and scooted next to the big girl and she put her arm around Crandall's neck. I swear to you, her arm was bigger than his upper leg. She said, invitingly, "Hi, I'm Sandra. What's your name?" Crandall spent the next five minutes attempting to maneuver his way back to the door. I was cracking up. Crandall looked back at me and asked "Have you seen my helmet, Bobby?" Then a moment later, he said "That's alright, Sandra was sitting on it." After a couple more minutes, Crandall managed to get his door opened. We exited the vehicle and told the ladies good night. About the same time, Sergeant Norton told us all that we were relieved for the day and we could go home. We got on our motors and I followed Crandall to the interstate. I have never seen him ride as fast as he did that night. The next day I asked him why he was riding so fast and he said, "I was afraid that hog was following me." He mentioned that he didn't believe what I had said about the girls being stewardesses. He said, "Sandra probably works at the airport but I'm guessing she pulls the planes onto the runway."

The downtown demonstration continued for several days and we remained on standby. When it finally ended, we had been working 16 hours a day for over a week. So on that last night, we decided to have a beer party at my house (I was single at the time). Sergeant Norton did not attend. He reminded us that we had an assignment the following morning to escort some dignitaries to the Agriculture Center. We assured him that we would be there bright and early. We then went to my house and about 5 a.m., the party broke up. We decided that we all needed a few hours sleep before our assignment. We were to be at a downtown motel at 10 a.m. I tried to persuade Crandall to stay at my house and catch a nap but he insisted on going to his house. He left as it was beginning to break daylight. Another officer was riding with

Crandall when they got to a dead end in the road where the other officer turned left and Marty went straight. He wrecked. His emergency lights were busted, his windshield was torn off and his motorcycle, which he kept in immaculate condition, was scratched from front to back. Anyway, Crandall got back on his motorcycle and headed home. He later said that when he pulled up to his garage, which was on the front of his house, his next door neighbor was outside watering his lawn. Marty said that when he attempted to open his garage door, he lost his balance and fell backwards, turning a back flip. He said his neighbor dropped his hose and began to applaud. Crandall went inside, his pants and shirt torn, and cuts all over his body. He covered the cuts with Merthiolate sat down in his chair and went to sleep.

  That morning, at 10 a.m. we were all at our assignment, that is, all but Crandall. The bus load of dignitaries was scheduled to leave at 10:30 a.m. Sergeant Norton got on the air and called Crandall several times. Finally he answered. "I'm on the way, sarge." About 10:10 a.m. Crandall arrived. He had not changed his clothes, he had not shaved and his motorcycle was still in the wrecked condition. Sergeant Norton decided to let him complete the assignment but told him to fall in to the rear. Crandall walked over and sat on the curb, his helmet in his lap. He looked worse than any homeless person you would encounter downtown. We got some pencils and put them in Crandall's helmet. Then, we stopped a pedestrian and asked him if he would drop some change into Crandall's helmet as if he were buying a pencil. He agreed to go along with the joke. The man walked over to Crandall and dropped the change into his helmet. The he said, "Just keep the pencil." Crandall, without looking up said, "God bless you sir." We all thanked the man for his participation.

At 10:30 a.m. the bus arrived and we started the escort. What we didn't know was that the person in charge of the tour had arranged for us to have lunch with the dignitaries. So around noon, we all went to the Agriculture Center cafeteria. Crandall happened to be seated across the table from the Mayor of one of the nearby cities. The Mayor took one look at Crandall and commented, "You guys must be having a tough time with those demonstrators." Crandall replied "Yes sir, it's a jungle out there."

Each September, it was customary for the traffic officers to work the State Fair. One such night created a humorous situation for Crandall, or might I say, humorous for every other officer there, except Crandall. This September night was a warm night and Crandall had taken his helmet off and placed it over the radio on his motorcycle. He saw a young lady walk in who had a reputation for being "police friendly." Crandall, feeling amorous, summoned her over and engaged in a conversation with her. Unbeknownst to him, his helmet had keyed the mike and everything he said was going out over the air. The conversation went something like this "Hey baby, come here a minute. You got time to give me a blow job? You don't know me? My name is Crandall. C-r-a-n-d-a-l-l." Well, one of the officers in the field was close to the fairgrounds and hurriedly headed towards the entrance to warn Crandall. The officer was a black officer assigned to the DUI testing squad. He parked his vehicle and as he was exiting the vehicle, Crandall spotted him and said to the young lady, "Wait a minute baby, and let me see what this nigger wants." This, of course, went out over the air and the black officer heard it loud and clear. Crandall then said to the black officer, "Hey what's up partner?" "Nothing" the black officer replied and then he got back into his vehicle and left. This is bad you say? Well, eventually Crandall took his helmet off the radio and another officer arrived and warned him. But that was not the worst of it, you see, Crandall's wife had a police scanner at their home and, as luck would have it, she was listening to it that September night. When Crandall got home, all his clothes had been thrown out of the house and onto the lawn.

Another story about Crandall also took place at the State Fairgrounds. One evening we were stationed inside the grounds near the racetrack entrance. The racetrack sits atop a hill where the outdoor stage shows were held. At the bottom of the hill, which had a very steep grade, was the midway. At the foot of the hill was a weight guessing stand. The prizes on
display were teddy bears – lots of teddy bears. You can imagine the crowd at the State Fair on a moonlit fall night. Anyway, at the top of the hill, there were some wheelchairs which were made available to the handicapped. As luck would have it, Crandall sat down on one of the wheelchairs and went sound asleep. We could not resist the temptation. We found some rope and bound Crandall to the chair, still

asleep. We turned Crandall towards the midway. We put his whistle in his mouth and launched the wheelchair. Crandall awoke and noting that he was moving and there were hundreds of people in his path, did what any conscientious officer would do. He started blowing his whistle. Now, Crandall was picking up speed and people were scattering to avoid being hit by a runaway wheelchair. Everyone was aware of the situation except one person. That's right, the man in the weight guessing stand. He had his back to the action and was busy arranging his teddy bears. By the time Crandall got to the bottom of the hill, he must have been doing at least 30 mph. He crashed into the stand, knocking the man down and tipping over the wheelchair. Teddy bears were airborne and came down landing on Crandall and the man. Crandall, never failing to come up with something clever to say, looked at the man and asked "Did you call the police?" As you can see, we were believers in the saying "all work and no play makes Jack a dull boy".

I don't want you to get the wrong impression though. We did work and we worked hard, but the play allowed us to keep our sanity.

Chapter IV

Fenamint Gum and Limburger Cheese

As I mentioned before, the traffic division provided a lot of fond memories. One such was a story related to me by Sergeant Norton. He had ridden motorcycles several years prior to our squad being formed with an officer named Harry Jamison. Harry, it's said, had a reputation for riding very fast. He lived in a hilly section in the suburbs. Harry was working the night shift one summer night and after being relieved, had sped off in the direction of his home. The next morning, a call came in to the chief's office.

The caller was an elderly lady who stated that one of his motorcycles was on her property. The chief assumed that one of his officers had his motorcycle quit on him and had left it on the lady's property. The chief informed the lady that he would send someone out to pick it up. The lady then said, "I don't think you fully understand, chief. The motorcycle is in the top of my tree." It seems that Harry had straightened out one of the curves on the way home and landed in tope of a tree. Unhurt, he got out of the tree and walked home. Miraculously, Harry did not have so much as a scratch on his body. The chief had to send a crane out to the lady's "tree" to retrieve the motor.

Another incident which, at the time, struck me funny involved Officer Gerald Bosworth. Officer Bosworth was one of those spit and polish officers who had a calm attitude about every situation. As motorcycle officers, we often were dispatched to accident scenes to conduct an investigation. On this particular occasion, Officer Bosworth had been dispatched to the scene of an accident involving two vehicles. One vehicle had slowed or stopped for a traffic light and the second vehicle had struck the first vehicle in the rear.

A simple report, right? Officer Bosworth parked his motorcycle behind the second vehicle and wrote the report. He issued the driver of the second vehicle a citation (ticket) for following too close. After informing the driver of his options, he advised both drivers that they could leave. As both vehicles pulled out into the traffic, the driver of the vehicle in front of Bosworth slowed. You guessed it. Bosworth hit the vehicle in the rear. He went down with his motorcycle pinning him to the pavement. The driver of
the vehicle which Bosworth had hit, got out of his vehicle and pulled the motorcycle off Bosworth. Then Officer Bosworth, after brushing himself off, asked the driver for the citation that he had issued to him. The driver handed it to him. Without saying anything, Bosworth tore the ticket in half, got on his motorcycle and rode off.

Before describing this next officer, I must tell you, if you haven't already surmised, the officers depicted here were, and still are, like family to me. I loved and respected all these guys. Now, let me introduce you to Officer Jerry Smith. Jerry was Mr. Nice. If he were your friend, you could not make him angry. If and when you played a joke on him, he would just smile and say "you got me." This "classic" happened one day when Jerry and I were assigned as catch men working radar. Another officer in an unmarked car would set up radar and we would pull our motorcycles off the side of the road about a block away. The officer in the radar car would call the vehicles out to us that were speeding and we would walk out into the street, pull them over and issue speeding tickets. We were working a busy street one day and were getting ready to get back to work after having lunch at Johnny's restaurant. On the handlebars of our motorcycles what we called "ditty bags". They were leather pouches which accommodated our ticket books, pens, etc. I usually kept a pack of Beeches chewing gum in there. Jerry had a habit of sneaking some of my gum when I wasn't looking.

Knowing this, I decided to get one on Jerry. I purchased a box of Fenamint (laxative) gum and got a box of Beeches and emptied it. I put the Fenamint gum inside. After setting up after lunch, the traffic thinned out and we weren't catching many speeders. Just as I had suspected, Jerry strolled over to my motor when he thought I wasn't looking and helped himself to some gum. After about 30 minutes, I guess the flavor of the gum wore off and Jerry helped himself to some more of my gum. In a few minutes, I went to my motor and took the gum out of my bag. I acted like I was upset and told Jerry, "Well, you've already chewed most of my gum Jerry. You might as well chew the rest." He smiled and said, "I'll get you some more, Bobby." He then chewed the remaining pieces. Jerry had chewed a total of seven pieces of laxative gum. Well, in about an hour, nature called. We were standing at the edge of the street when all of a sudden Jerry said, "Oops" and started towards his motor. I said "Where are you going Jerry?" "I

gotta go, Bobby." I grabbed Jerry's arm and said "You can't leave Jerry, we're working radar." "Let go of me, Bobby, I gotta go." With that, Jerry got on his motorcycle and sped off toward the nearest service station two blocks away. In about 30 minutes, he came back. He was pale. He got off
his motor and slowly walked over to me saying, "Sorry Bobby, but I had to go bad." He said it must have been something he ate at Johnny's Restaurant.

Our shift was about over and we would now go to headquarters. Jerry asked that I turn in his paperwork for him because he was going home. The next day, Jerry came to work and he looked very pale and weak. He said, "You know I went to the bathroom seven times last night." He told me that he and his wife had gone to a dance that night and that a pain hit him right in the middle of a dance with a friend. I asked "What did you do, Jerry?" "I told her to excuse me and I ran to the bathroom." He said that he just barely made it. As I said, Jerry was a good natured guy but I never did tell him what I had done. I don't know if he suspected anything or not but he never stole my gum again.

I mentioned Johnny's Restaurant before. Well, as you probably know, police officers usually have a restaurant on each side of town that they frequent. Johnny's was the restaurant on the northeast side of town. One summer day several of the "squad" was having lunch at Johnny's. One of the officers, and I won't mention which one, decided to get Jerry again. He got a piece of limburger cheese and while Jerry was busy eating, put the cheese on the block of Jerry's motorcycle. Well, we left and Jerry and I were riding together. It was a very warm summer day and after a few minutes the cheese melted. Jerry motioned for me to pull over. I did so and Jerry said "something's wrong with my motor Bobby." I asked what he thought the problem was and he said he didn't know. He got off his motor and walked around with this puzzled look, shaking his head. He said he thought maybe a wire was burning. He asked me to see if I could smell anything. After taking a close look, I told him I couldn't smell anything unusual. It was all I could do not to gag. The odor was horrible. Think of the worse smell that you have ever sensed. Well, this was ten times worse. Anyway, we rode off again. After about 30 minutes, Jerry pulled over and said he was going to call the sergeant. He said he was afraid he was going to damage his motor by continuing to ride. Sergeant Norton showed up in about five minutes. Jerry asked, "Sarge will you ride my motor and see if you think anything is wrong with it?" He told Sergeant Norton that he smelled a foul odor. Sergeant Norton, after noting a smile from me, got on Jerry's motor and took off. In a couple minutes he came back and I could see his eyes were watering. He got off and informed Jerry, "No, I didn't smell anything, Jerry." The sergeant later told me he thought he was going to pass out when he rode Jerry's motor.

We tried to convince Jerry that he probably had a sinus infection and that he apparently smelled something we couldn't smell. The foul odor remained a mystery to Jerry.

Our sergeant was not exempt from being the victim in a funny story either. He told this one on himself. He was working the day shift when he was dispatched to one of the larger churches in the city to escort a funeral. He said that as he approached the church he could see what he estimated to be two or three hundred people outside the church. The services were being held for one of the prominent citizens and a lot of dignitaries were in attendance. He admitted that he was kind of showing off as he came closer to the crowd. He said that he was riding pretty fast and as he got to the front of the church, he slid the back end of the motorcycle around by locking his back brakes. He then backed the motor to the curb, cut the engine, threw his right leg over and assumed a side saddle position. He felt proud that he had stopped so impressively and every eye was focused on his feat. He only made one mistake – he forgot to put his kickstand down. In an instant the mood changed from proud to helpless. The motorcycle took him to the pavement pinning him beneath almost 1,000 pounds of the Harley Davidson "Hog". The good sergeant did the only thing he could at the moment. He summoned some of the men in the crowd and said, "If a couple of you gentlemen would kindly get this motorcycle off me, I'll be glad to escort the procession for you." They did so and he did, too.

One year, while working the State Fair, there was a large fire that erupted in one of the buildings. Sergeant Norton quickly got on the radio and sent us all to assignments advising us to get the crowd out of the area and to safety. We did so and with the help of the Fire Department and other officers, remarkably, there were no deaths or serious injuries to the fair goers.

Soon after this, the Mayor held a ceremony honoring those who were working the fair on the night of the fire. Of course, our motorcycle squad was among the honorees.

We all lined up in formation and sped onto the race track which was in front of the grandstands. The ceremony lasted about an hour or so and several speakers, including the Mayor paid tribute to us and the others involved in getting all to safety that night.

When it was over, Sergeant Norton gave the signal to start our engines. The Harleys, at that time had a kick starter. Well, as luck would have it, everyone started their motorcycles on the first kick, everyone except me. I kicked it several times to no avail. Finally, Sergeant Norton, seeing that I couldn't get my motor started, gave the signal to exit. There were thousands of people watching this.

As all, but me, pulled off, there I was, all alone. Then, a miracle occurred. My Harley finally fired up. I pulled off by myself and the crowd gave me a standing ovation. My face, I know, was bright red and when I got to the rest of the squad, they all applauded me. That kind of attention, I sure didn't need.

I know you're all familiar with the Shriners. Well, one week, they held their convention in Nashville and our squad was assigned to the traffic downtown. They had a parade one night and, of course, Officer Crandall was there with his usual but unusual antics.

The parade was viewed by thousands and it was a memorable night for all. Well, all but one. That's right, Officer Crandall. Seems one of the Shriners talked Crandall into swapping motorcycles. Do you know about these tiny motorcycles that you see in the parades? A group of Shriners do maneuvers on them and everyone, especially the children, enjoy their display.

Anyway, Crandall agreed to swap motorcycles and ended up riding this mini-motorcycle the rest of the night. He hadn't planned to ride it all night but the Shriner never returned Crandall's motorcycle and he couldn't find him.

When it came time to return to headquarters at the end of our shift, we all got there except Crandall. Sergeant Norton was waiting at the entrance to headquarters and finally, Crandall comes riding up on the mini-motorcycle. His knees were spread and up in the air as he arrived.

Sergeant Norton could not believe what he was seeing. He walked over to Crandall and said, "What happened to your motorcycle, Crandall?" Crandall, without hesitation, responded, "I don't know Sergeant, I guess it shrunk."

Later that night the Shriner came to headquarters with Crandall's motorcycle.

Chapter V

The Bird-Brained Burglar and the Monkey and the Cat

It was 1968. Jacqueline Kennedy marries Greek magnate Aristotle Onassis. Afro haircuts become popular among black men. And, my tour in the traffic division ends. On a snowy night in January, two of my brother officers were gunned down. The officers had been working "one officer cars" in a high crime area. Several of the traffic officers were temporarily transferred to the patrol division in order to double up in the zones. I was among those transferred.

After working in patrol for a couple months, I decided that I would be better satisfied staying there. I requested an official transfer and was granted such. Our department was now acquiring air conditioned cars. We all considered this a luxury. We were also getting mace. The latter became a great inspiration to lock your police vehicle when on a call. You see, some of the guys started going by the scene of calls and if the officers on call had not locked their vehicles, the pranksters would leave a lasting gift – mace. As I said, shortly after being issued mace, we all learned to lock our vehicles when left unattended.

    I was now working out of the west sector and assigned to a car with Officer Sandy Barnes. Sandy would later become one of my sergeants in the Vice Squad. We are assigned to a zone which bordered the Cumberland River and the interstate crossed the Cumberland near downtown. Sandy and I were working the midnight shift one summer night. We had just gotten a new device in our patrol car – an intercom. Needless to say, it had become somewhat of a toy for some of the officers. Anyway, it was about 3 a.m. when we heard the midnight traffic car receive a 10-46 call, an accident involving injury on the

Silliman-Evans Bridge (the bridge that crossed the river). After the traffic car (212) arrived on the scene, the officers noticed that the guard rail was broken. Traffic Officer Sumpter requested that a zone car be sent to the road below the bridge to check for a possible vehicle involved in their wreck call. I might add here that the traffic division at that

time had a false sense that they were "above" the patrol division. So, we kinda resented their asking the "lowly" patrol officers to assist them in their dirty work. In any event, we checked the river bank directly under the bridge. We advised the dispatcher there was nothing unusual there. Traffic car 212 then radioed, "We'll go down there and check it." This infuriated Sandy. So, he backed our car in between two buildings and waited. In a few minutes car 212 arrived and the officers began shining their spotlights up and down the river bank. As I mentioned, we had a new intercom speaker in our car and Sandy picked up the mike and as we sat there camouflaged by the darkness, transmitted on the intercom. "Help we're in the river. Help. Help."

Officer Sumpter in 212 came back over the air, "212 to headquarters. We've got one in the river. We can hear them calling for help." Then all hell broke loose. The captain on duty got into the act. "Get a boat in the river right away." 212 radioed, "See if you can get a scuba diver on the scene." I looked at Sandy and said, "I wish you hadn't done that shit." Sandy was panicking. "Oh shit. We'll get fired if they find out it was us they heard." "What the hell do you mean us?" I fired back. 212 was still shining their lights near the river bank. They were about 300 yards away. Sandy headed towards them in a panic. We pulled up beside them and Sandy said, "Hey guys that was us on the PA." Officer Sumpter, I have to admit, thought fast. "212 to headquarters. Tell all cars to signal 9 (disregard). We found where the voice was coming from – it was a cat with his head hung in a bottle." The traffic guys had saved us from a lot of embarrassment and maybe even a suspension. After thinking about Officer Sumpter's quick thinking though, I realized that the explanation of the cat with his head in a jar was a flimsy excuse. How could a cat make that that much noise if his head was inside a bottle? Oh well, it worked anyway, Sandy wasn't as eager to play with his new toy after that experience.

    One of my partners at the west sector was Officer Jim Burns. Jim was a short, muscular guy who would fight a tiger with you if need be. We felt comfortable working together, each know that if, as they say, the shit hit the fan, the other would be there. We used to do this thing when we stopped a man on a minor traffic violation. Jim would go to the vehicle and in his "gay voice" ask for the man's driver's license. He would say things like "What is wrong with you, you silly thing? You were just flying down that silly ole street." After just a couple minutes, about nine out of ten drivers would ask to speak to his partner.

Jim would then motion to me. I would walk to the vehicle and in my gay voice say, "What in the world is taking you so long? Are you going to write this big guy a ticket or what?" Then, Jim would hand the license back to the driver and say, "Just go on. I just don't want to talk to you anymore." We would get back in our car and die laughing. One night we picked up this regular drunk off the street. We put him in the back seat and headed towards booking. Jim looked over at him and in his gay voice said, "He's kinda cute, isn't he?" I suggested to him "Why don't we just go park with this good looking thing." Jim said, "Let's go." The drunk went ballistic. He said, "You two fag mother-fuckers take me to jail. If you stop this car, I'll kick both your fag asses." Jim looked at me and said excitedly, "I just love it when they get physical." We took the drunk to booking and when we went before the judge to obtain the warrant, the drunk told the judge "I got one thing to say judge." "Yes, what is it?" "You need to get rid of these two queers judge." We just looked at his honor and shrugged in a, we don't know what he's talking about, gesture.

One of the funniest situations I recall actually happened in another state. Officer Harold Collins and I had become "off duty" buddies. Officer Collins was sworn in six months after I became an officer. He was an avid race car fan and persuaded me to go with him to a race in Talladega, Alabama. The race was on a Sunday. Harold had constructed a stand which we transported on top of his car. When we arrived, we parked in the infield and got on top of the car to view the race. We had a cooler full of "refreshments". During the race, a man walked over to our car and handed Harold a note. The note read, "Could we buy a six pack from you? They aren't selling it here and we ran out." Harold took the pen from the man and wrote a reply. It read, "Here, no charge." He handed the man a six pack. Well, Harold and the man continued to write notes to each other throughout the race. It was apparent that the man could not speak or hear. We continued to indulge from the cooler. Just before the end of the race, Harold wrote a final note to the man. It read, "If you're ever in Nashville and want to go to the Grand Ole Opry, call me at this number." Harold put his home phone number on the note. The man, after reading the note, shook Harold's hand and nodded the affirmative. Well, first of all, I thought why a man who could not hear would want to go to the Grand Ole Opry. And, if by some strange reason, he decided to go, how in the hell could he call Harold on the phone?

Now getting back to the Police Department, I recall a funny situation staring Officer Billy Dunn. It seems Billy had a girlfriend who lived with her boyfriend in Billy's zone. The young lady told Billy that her boyfriend was very jealous. The boyfriend worked the night shift which provided Billy the opportunity to visit this "lady of the night". On one such visit, Billy was inside the residence when, as luck would have it, the boyfriend came home unexpectedly. Not wanting to have a confrontation, Billy exited by way of the bedroom window. He began running towards his partner who was parked nearby. The boyfriend got a glimpse of Billy and began a foot pursuit. Billy made it to the patrol car and hurriedly got inside. He told his partner, frantically, "Let's go". The boyfriend got in his car and started after the patrol car. Both vehicles pulled onto the main road and the boyfriend was gaining on them. Not knowing what else to do, Billy reached over and turned on the emergency lights. His partner followed the lead by turning on the siren. The boyfriend continued the pursuit. Now imagine this – a police car is going down a busy street with emergency equipment on and directly behind there's a private vehicle directly behind it and the driver is firing a weapon at the police car. Quite a reversal of roles I would say, right? In any event, Billy and his partner lost the boyfriend and I was told that Billy's relationship with the young lady ended that night.

Now allow me to tell you about an encounter which involved my partner, Tony Kinnard, and me. Tony was originally from New York. He was a brash talking guy who, as Howard Cosell would say, would "tell it like it is". Tony and I received a call in an upscale section of the city. The call was put out as a possible burglary in progress. On arrival, we were met at the driveway by a middle-aged lady. She stated that someone was inside her residence. She said that she had come home from shopping and when entering, heard someone upstairs. We told her to stay outside and we entered the residence. After checking the downstairs, we cautiously headed upstairs. The only sound we could hear was the sound of our breathing. As we arrived at the top of the stairs, we observed a long hall which led from one end of the house to the other end. There were three doors on each side of the hallway. Tony took the left side and I took the right.

First, I opened my door. There was no one inside the room. Now, it was Tony who opened a door. The silence was broken by a very loud SQUAWK. We both, instinctively, raised our weapons to the ready position. Tony was waiving his revolver in a circular motion at the biggest parrot I have ever seen. The parrot was flying around the room and making more noise than a 747. Tony finally realizing what we had encountered quickly closed the door. We checked the rest of the house and went downstairs and out of the residence to meet with the lady. Tony walked over to the complainant and said, "Lady, I almost killed your damn bird." After talking with her for a few minutes, we concluded that the parrot had gotten out of his cage while she was away and when she returned, she heard the parrot bumping against the walls upstairs. Tony and I labeled that the case of the bird brained burglar.

At this point, I have to mention a couple of my fellow officers who were the recipients of a prestigious award. The Police Department had an award called "The Odd Fellows Award." This award was given for the best criminal case stemming from a routine traffic stop.

We were on the midnight shift and Officers Carl Gatewood and Kenneth Gant were partners assigned to car 42 downtown. At roll call this particular night, the lieutenant had stressed to all the importance of writing some traffic tickets. Well, around 3 a.m. Officers Gatewood and Gant, who had not made any traffic stops when Gatewood was driving, noticed an out-of-state vehicle run a traffic light. Gatewood shook Gant who was slouched down in the car seat. Seems that shift had been eventless and Gant was getting kinda sleepy. Anyway, Gatewood told Gant, "Here's our chance Kenneth. That car just ran the light and it's out-of-state. We can get a ticket and an arrest at one stop." You see, back then, if you wrote a ticket to a person from another state, you had to "book" that person and get the fine up front. Of course, he or she could return on the court date for a hearing but very few did. Gatewood hit the siren and lights and pulled the car over. He got out of the patrol car and walked to the driver's side of the vehicle. The car was occupied by one white male in his late 30's Gant, still half asleep, stayed in the patrol car because the male white was talking non-stop. When Gatewood asked the driver if he knew why he was stopped, you won't believe what happened next. The driver said, "I guess your partner is running my tag and you're gonna find out that this is a stolen car. Then I guess, you're gonna run my name on the drivers license and you'll find out that I'm wanted in Texas for armed robbery and murder." Gatewood then motioned for Gant to get out of the patrol car. Gant reluctantly got out and walked to Gatewood and the driver of the vehicle. Gatewood told Gant, "Kenneth, he just admitted that this car is stolen and he's wanted for armed robbery and murder in Texas." Gant took the cue and said, "Yeah, I was just checking the tag when you signaled." They immediately put the guy in search position and began the search incident to arrest when the guy said, "Well, you might as well go ahead and search the trunk. That's where I have 5,000 amphetamines." Now for those who aren't familiar with amphetamines, or commonly known as "speed", one of the effects they have on a person is they make you talk a lot. So, I'm assuming that this guy had taken several of the pills before he was stopped.

After handcuffing the guy and putting him in the back seat of the patrol car, Officer Gant radioed headquarters and said, "We've got a subject on a traffic stop. Give me a listing and stolen on the following tag number." Gant gave the dispatcher the tag number. "Then check the following subject for warrants and stops." Needless to say Gant and Gatewood were delighted when the dispatcher said, in an excited voice, "Car 42, do you have the subject under control?" "10-4, we do," replied Gant. The dispatcher then told the officers that the vehicle was stolen and the subject was wanted for robbery and murder in Texas. "10-4, car 42, we have also confiscated several thousand amphetamines." With great pride, Gatewood and Gant transported the subject to headquarters after towing the vehicle to the tow-in-lot. And, after the sergeant reminded them of the Odd Fellows Award, they wrote a brief description of the "traffic stop." They won the quarterly award and were given certificates and $150.00 to divide. When asked about the arrest by fellow officers, they just replied, "Just shows what hard work will get you." Yeah, right.

The next episode occurring while working at the west sector was what I call "monkeying around". This involved a routine call which normally would be handled by the fire department but we were fortunate in receiving the call concerning a pet monkey up a tree. The call was given to Officers Sandy Barnes and Bobby Fortner. Upon arrival, a somewhat frantic lady informed the officers that her pet monkey was in a tree in her front yard and she could not coax him down. As they were conversing, Sergeant Barnett arrived. Now Sergeant Barnett seemed to be able to handle almost any emergency in stride. So, when he pulled up to the scene, he was briefed by Barnes and Fortner. They told him that they were unsure how to get the monkey out of the tree. Sergeant Barnett told the officers to see if they could find a cat at one of the homes nearby. Puzzled, but not questioning the sergeant's order, they walked to the homes on each side of the monkey's home and inquired about a cat. Soon, Officer Fortner appeared with a cat from next door. Sergeant Barnett told him to put the cat at the base of the tree and walk away. Fortner complied and placed the black and white cat on the ground near the base of the tree and walked away. As Fortner walked over to Sergeant Barnett and Barnes, he noticed the monkey looking down at the cat. The monkey slowly descended from the top of the tree, jumped down on the cat and mounted it. The cat let out a blood curdling sound. The monkey hunched on the cat for several seconds and then released it. The cat raced to its home next door. Almost immediately after, a lady from the house came running towards the officers shouting, "What happened to my cat?" About this time, there was a loud boom echoed from the base of the tree. Officer Barnes, noting that the monkey was rapidly climbing back up the tree, shot it with his 12 gauge shotgun. Now the owner of the cat and the monkey were screaming hysterically. Sergeant Barnett told Barnes and Fortner to go to their cars and check back in (leave). I wasn't privy to the conversation between Sergeant Barnett and the two ladies but he had to explain why the monkey got shot and the cat got screwed. He must have been successful for there never was a formal complaint filed. I told you he could handle any emergency in stride.

Before I tell you about my transfer to vice, I would like to share with you a story about Red Stanton. Red was one of those guys who was very "goosey". You could walk up behind Red, goose him, and say something to him. He would repeat whatever you said. But, he wouldn't just repeat what you said, he would shout it. One day we were at roll call and the lieutenant was reading some orders which had come from the chief. After reading the first order, the Lieutenant stated, "That came from the chief". Well, someone goosed Red and whispered, "Fuck the chief". Red shouted "Fuck the chief". We all roared. As the laughter grew, I happened to glance over at the entrance door and standing just inside the roll call room was none other than that's right, the Chief of Police. The laughter gradually ceased as more and more officers discovered the chief's presence. Then the chief casually walked to the podium and said, in a sincere tone, "I don't know how many of you share Red's suggestion, but let me tell you all, you can forget it".

Chapter VI

Vice Squad, Copping Cocaine and Watermelons

DEA Training New Orleans 1973

It's 1971. Hot pants, shag haircuts and miniskirts arrive on the scene. Our police department is increasing in size. We're getting female officers out in the field. And, gambling, drugs and prostitution are escalating. I requested, and was granted, a transfer to Vice. Tony was also going. Our captain was Raymond Marrow. Our lieutenant was Richard Oldham. We had three sergeants, each having a squad of four officers. One of the sergeants, Tony Caldwell, told a story which occurred a year or so before my transfer.

Tony had a friend, Jerry Saindon, who worked at a health club in the suburbs. Tony knew that this club did not have any black members. So, he talked one of the black vice officers into calling Saindon. The black officer, Marcus Jones, called Jerry and, in his southern, black voice, inquired about becoming a member. Of course, Jerry said that he would have to take the information and log it for future consideration. He told Marcus that the club was not accepting any new members at the present but as soon as there was a vacancy, he would be contacted. Marcus was calling from the Vice office and Tony was recording the conversation. After an hour or so, Marcus called back. "Mr. Saindon, this is Marcus Jones." "Yes, Mr. Jones, how can I help you?" "You know after we hung up, I got to thinking. I am sure you know that I'm black, don't you?" "No sir, I didn't, but that wouldn't make any difference anyway." "Well, I think it would. In fact, I think that's the only reason you put me off is because I'm black." "No sir, I told you there's a waiting list right now." "Well, I think that's bullshit. I don't believe you have a waiting list." "Now wait a minute. I don't appreciate you calling me and cursing. I told you that I would call you if we have an opening." "Well, I want you to give me a membership in your club and I want you to give it to me today." "I told you, we're full right now but when we have an opening, I'll consider you." "What do you mean, you'll consider me?" "Just what I said, I'll consider you. We have other people wanting to be members also." "Ha! I thought so. You're not gonna let me in just because I'm black, are you, honky?" "You kiss my ass. Ain't no way I'd let your black ass in now." "I told you, you were a prejudiced asshole. I'm gonna come out there and kick your white ass." "Well, come on mother-fucker. When you get here I got something for your ass." "Oh yeah, what you got, honky?" "It's called Mr. 38, mother-fucker." Both parties then hung up abruptly.

In about 30 seconds, the Vice phone rang. It was Saindon. "Thank God you're in, Tony. I need you to get out here quick. Some crazy black guy is on his way out here to kick my ass and I don't even have a gun." "What happened?" "I don't have time to explain, Tony. Just get out here quick." "Okay Jerry, just keep the door locked, we'll be there shortly." Tony and Marcus, along with four other vice officers, drove to the club. Marcus, who by the way was a big guy, got out of the car and went to the door. He had this serious look on his face when he knocked. Saindon was seated behind a desk and appeared to be the only person inside. He ignored the knock. About this time, Tony and the other officers stepped up to the door beside Marcus. Jerry, seeing that the cavalry had arrived, ran to the door and unlocked it. "That's him, Tony. Lock the mother-fucker up. I'll sign the warrant." Marcus, along with all the other officers, started laughing. Jerry had been got good. A couple years later, Jerry become a police officer and was assigned to Vice after graduating from the academy. Of course, he had to hear the taped conversation between Marcus and him almost daily.

Shortly after being transferred to Vice, Captain Marrow called all five new vice officers in. He told us that we would be going to the DEA (Drug Enforcement Administration) school in New Orleans for a two week course. After making the necessary arrangements, we were assigned vehicles to use for transportation. Since most of the undercover vehicles that we used were old, Captain Marrow allowed us to take his police car and Lieutenant Oldham's car. Captain Marrow called Frank and me in and gave us a briefing on the use of his police car. He told us not to drive it (a new Chevrolet) over 70 mph. He emphasized this, warning that the fan belt would come off at any speed above 70. We, of course, assured him that we would keep his car under 70. We left Nashville early one morning with the three other officers leading the way. Somewhere around Jackson, Tennessee, which is about 120 miles from Nashville, we got separated from the other officers. In an effort to catch them, I increased our speed considerably. All of a sudden, I saw the emergency lights in my rear view mirror. It was the Highway Patrol. I slowed and pulled over to the side of the interstate. The trooper walked to our car and asked for my driver's license. I got out of the car and retrieved my license and handed them to the trooper. He requested that I walk to the front of the vehicle. I did so, and he placed my license on the hood. I took out my police ID and placed it on the hood beside my license. I thought surely he would see the police ID and not issue a ticket. I knew I was speeding and he corroborated this by saying, "I clocked you at 92 mph." He then took out his ticket book and began to write. I said, wondering now if he had seen my ID, "You know, we're on our way to New Orleans to attend the DEA drug school." He replied, "You ought to be going to driving school." I was thinking, not only is he going to write me a ticket but he's going to be a smart ass, also. About this time, the wind stirred and the license and ID blew off the hood. He looked at the ID and asked, "Are you a police officer?" "We sure are", I replied. He handed me the ticket and said, "You guys be careful". I asked if he wanted the ticket and he said not to worry, he would get his copies voided. I put the ticket in the glove box and we were back on our way to New Orleans. We gathered a lot of knowledge about drugs while there but we should have remembered something about evidence. In a couple of days after going back to work, Capitan Marrow called me to his office. When I walked in, he was holding the ticket in his hand. He said, "Can you explain this, Officer Bass?" Well, I should have been given an A-plus for fast thinking. I just started laughing. "Frank and I said we'd like to be there when you found that, Captain. We got a trooper to write that when we stopped in Jackson to eat." I guess he believed me because if he hadn't, I probably still wouldn't be able to sit after he got through chewing.

I learned very fast that the Vice Squad, much like the Motorcycle Squad, had an abundance of practical jokers. Being new in the squad, I suppose I had to be initiated. This was accomplished on or about my third week in Vice. Lieutenant Oldham called me to his office one night. In the office, with the Lieutenant, was Sergeant Foster Hale. Sergeant Hale grew up in my old neighborhood and was a guy I trusted implicitly. So I didn't hesitate when he informed me that he had a "buy" set up and wanted me to make it. He said that a snitch of his had set up the buy. I was to go to one of the suburban shopping centers at 8 p.m. and stand in front of this particular window display. A male white, in his 30s, about 5' 10" 190 lbs. would be there. The code word would be "expensive". When the seller saw me looking at the window display, he would walk over to me and say the code word. My reply would be "You can afford it", and then the deal would go down. I would be copping cocaine and it would be a sizeable buy. The lieutenant emphasized that I should be careful with the buy money. So, after going over the plan with my backup, I headed to the shopping center and got there about 7:30 p.m. I walked over to the window and looked at the display. Shortly after my arrival, I could see a male white out of the corner of my eye. He had a handkerchief over his mouth and was sniffing frequently. I thought to myself, "This guy's on the shit bad." He slowly walked over next to me and while we both gazed at the display, said "Expensive". "You can afford it," I replied. With that, he said, "You got the cash?" "Yeah, you got the stuff?" He then took a baggie out of his coat pocket and I could see that it contained a white substance. At almost the same time, we exchanged. I walked back to my car, not looking back, and left.

I radioed to my backup and told them to signal me at headquarters. I went to Lieutenant Oldham's office and was met there by Lieutenant Oldham, Sergeant Hale, and six vice officers. I handed the baggie to Sergeant Hale. He had a test kit on his desk. He took a sample of the substance and dropped it into one of the vials. Then, he got this serious look on his face and started shaking his head in a negative way. Lieutenant Oldham said, "What is it, sergeant?" "I don't know, lieutenant, but it's not coke. You got ripped off, Bobby". "I'll be a son-of-a-bitch." Lieutenant Oldham then began to raise hell about my losing the buy money by being ripped off. I was getting real concerned, especially when he said that the captain was going to hit the ceiling when he found out about the blunder. Then I got the clue that I needed. I glanced over at Sergeant Hale and he was smiling. I knew then that I had been set up. I decided to do a little impromptu act of my own. I jumped up from my chair and said angrily, "I'm going back out there, lieutenant and when I find that shit head, he's a dead mother-fucker." With that, I left the office almost in a dead run. Lieutenant Oldham was right behind me. "Wait a minute, Bobby. We were just playing with you." I stopped and broke out in laughter. "I knew that all along, Lieutenant." Yeah, I thought, I knew it right after I saw the sergeant smile. After that, Lieutenant Oldham and I got along great. We seemed to have bonded. I found him to be an outstanding supervisor. Did I mention that he was black? Well, knowing this will allow you to see the humor in the next situation.

One of the officers who transferred to Vice when I did, was Officer Donny Wainwright. Donny was a short man of stature but had the energy of three men. If you suggested, Donny let's go lock up every drug dealer in the city, Donny would reply, "Let's go." Anyway, Donny had a good heart and would die before hurting another officer's feelings. One night, Lieutenant Oldham, who I mentioned, was black, came to work and was exceptionally cheerful. After getting our assignments for the night, the lieutenant announced that we would knock off an hour early that night. "What for" inquired Donny. "Well, Donny, today is my birthday, and we're gonna celebrate." "Great," answered Donny. "Let's get a watermelon." We all broke out in laughter. That is except the lieutenant and Donny. The lieutenant, knowing Donny, and sensing an opportunity to get him, just shook his head and walked out of the office. Donny frantically went after him. "Wait a minute, lieutenant. I didn't mean anything." Donny, walking behind the lieutenant, said, "I just thought it's a warm night and a watermelon would be good." "That's alright, Donny, I know exactly what you meant." Then, the lieutenant went outside, got in his car, and drove off. Donny came inside and went to each officer apologizing. "I didn't mean anything, really." We each told Donny, "I think you fucked up, Donny. The lieutenant was really hurt." After awhile, I began to feel sorry for Donny. So, I was relieved to see the lieutenant walk back in. He was laughing. He walked over and gave Donny a pat on the back. "That was the funniest thing I ever heard, Donny." Donny was relieved. After that, we had a standard response when anyone announced they were having a birthday. "Great, let's get a watermelon."

Chapter VII

The Fireside Fart, the Drug Raid and Frogman

Sergeant Hale was the contributor of my next humorous event. We, Sergeant Hale, Officer Pringle and I, were sent by the captain to talk with this lady about her son. It seems that she was concerned that he might be experimenting with drugs. She lived in an affluent section and when we arrived at her residence, we were greeted by a maid. We were escorted to the "den" which was a gigantic room with this huge fireplace. The furnishings were so expensive looking that we declined to sit when invited to do so. We were standing with our backs to the fireplace and this aristocratic-looking lady was standing facing us. About five minutes into her conversation, which was directed primarily toward Sergeant Hale, there was a moment of silence. That's when it happened – Sergeant Hale let the loudest fart I have ever heard. Well, with his back to this huge fireplace, the acoustics were just right. The fart crescendoed into a long echo. I could not control my reaction. I started laughing hysterically. Realizing that I couldn't allow myself the embarrassment of the moment, I changed my laughter to an uncontrollable cough. I started towards the door and Sergeant Hale said, "Officer Bass has a terrible cold, you'll have to excuse him." The lady either didn't hear the fart, which I find very hard to believe, or, she just chose to ignore it. I choose to believe the latter. In fact, I believe the next door neighbor probably heard the sound that I later labeled "the fireside fart".

Another officer I enjoyed working with in vice was Officer Jim Cain. Jim was a tall, lanky black officer who could give you the most serious look you have ever seen. He could get anyone's attention simply by looking that person in the eye. One summer night Jim and

I were cruising one of the high drug traffic areas, a business district in the predominantly black part of town. As we passed this corner where a lot of drug sales were known to go down, Jim suddenly said, "Stop the car Bobby". He got out of the car and walked over to this male black subject who was standing on the corner. Now this guy was really decked out. He was standing in front of the local pool hall and was apparently being admired by all. The area was heavily congested with pedestrian traffic. I got out of the car and stood beside the driver's door covering Jim. He walked over to this guy who was dressed in his "super fly" outfit and said "take off the shoes". I knew that a lot of street dealers kept their stash in their shoes so this request did not surprise me. "Naw, Jim, not the shoes" replied the guy. Then Jim got real demanding. "Give me the fucking shoes". The guy reluctantly took off the shoes and handed them to Jim. Jim got back in the car and said "let's go, Bobby". After we pulled off, I glanced in my rear view mirror and I could see Mr. Super Fly standing on the corner in his stocking feet. Everyone was looking at his feet and laughing. He was offering some lame excuse to the "brothers" on the corner as to why he gave up his shoes. I asked Jim what was going on. He said "I sold these shoes to that mother-fucker and he didn't pay me. I'm repossessing them." I would guess that the shoeless guy's reputation plummeted to an all time low that night.

As I said, Jim could get a real serious look on his face which sometimes was frightening. One such example occurred one night when he and I confronted this drug dealer on a busy corner. During the conversation, which became somewhat heated, the guy made the mistake of calling Jim a "nasty nigger". Jim grabbed the guy by the collar and, picked him up off the ground, looked him right in the eye and said, "don't you ever call me that again, mother-fucker." I, of course, assumed that Jim was offended by the "N" word. He then said to the guy, still holding him off the ground, "my ass is cleaner than your mama ever got yours when you were a baby so don't ever call me nasty again. You got that mother fucker?" The guy, of course said, "Yes sir". We got in our car and as we were leaving, Jim looked at me and said, "Can you imagine that shit head calling me nasty?" "I sure can't Jim," I replied. I guess I was right after all. Jim had been offended by the "N" word with the "N" word being nasty.

Remember Tony Kinnard the case of the bird-brained burglar? Well, as I mentioned, Tony went to vice the same time I did. We all developed informants. Tony had one who put him on a duplex on the south side of town. The informant told Tony that heroin was being sold at a particular address. We went by the residence and got a description of the duplex in question. The informant had told Tony that the drugs were being sold out of the left side of the duplex. We got the search warrant and took Officer Kenneth Gant with us. Upon arriving, we could see that someone was looking out of the window beside the front door. We went to the door immediately and announced our presence. Tony said "Police Department, we have a search warrant for this residence. Open up". The person, who had been looking out the window, let the shade all the way up and we could see it was a white female in her 50s. She said, "You're not the cops." With that, Tony took out his I.D. and held it to the window. Officer Gant walked over to the door and, surprisingly, it was unlocked. We all three entered. Well, the lady started screaming. She sounded like ten sirens going off at one time. Tony stayed with her while Kenneth and I checked the rest of the residence for other occupants. We didn't find anyone. The lady kept screaming "Help! Help! Somebody call the police." Tony was trying to assure her that we were the police but she would have none of that. She just kept screaming. In a few minutes, a neighborhood lady walked to the front yard. The lady who was screaming said "call the police, Helen" and the lady left the yard. Finally the lady apparently was accepting the fact that we weren't going to harm her and she stopped screaming. Tony informed her that we were going to search her residence and that she should sit in her chair and remain calm. She did so, until looking out the window, saw a police car stop in front of her residence. She jumped up and ran towards the door. Tony was in hot pursuit. They both ran out onto the porch with the lady screaming, "Help police. They're trying to kill me". The officers in the police car saw Tony on the porch and recognizing him as an officer, pulled off. When the lady saw the police car leaving, she went berserk. "Oh no, don't leave" she screamed. Then, you could tell she was getting angry. "You bastards, you're never around when I need you. Go on you mother-fuckers." With Tony herding her along, she finally went back inside. We again showed her our I.D.s and learned that her name was Miss Dorman. She sat back down on her chair and began to critique our search. "You're not gonna find anything you dumb son-of-a bitch." "Lady, I'm not dumb" said Tony. At one point, Kenneth handed a bottle to Tony which contained small white pills. The lady spoke up and said "They're gonna laugh at you when you send that to the lab, you dumb mother-fuckers. Those are saccharin tablets." We finally finished the search and after reassuring the lady that we wouldn't be back, left the premises. We learned later that Tony's informant had given us the wrong side of the duplex. About a month later, Tony and I stopped at a pizza restaurant on the east side of town. When we went inside, we saw, no other than, Miss Dorman behind the counter. Needless to say, we turned around and made a quick exit.

Another officer I had the privilege to work within Vice was Officer Stan Morton. Stan was an intelligent guy who was raised in a well-to-do section of the city. He was a sort of young looking Robert Redford. He did, however, have a good sense of humor. He had this little joke that he would play on non-suspecting individuals. It required the assistance of a couple officers to set it up. We decided to play the joke on Donny. Remember Donny, Mr. "Watermelon" man? Here's how the joke went. We would all be sitting around the office when Stan was not present. One of us said, "Well, Stan's talking about his sister again." Another officer would say "yeah, he's wearing my ass out talking about her." That's how the joke got started. One night, Tony, Kenneth, Donny and I were sitting around and I said "Stan's started that shit with his sister again." Tony said, "yeah, I'm getting tired hearing that bullshit." Donny asked, "What are you talking about?" "You haven't heard Stan bragging about his sister" I replied? "I don't know what you're talking about." I explained to Donny that Stan had a sister who was a dancer. "Well, Stan thinks she's some kind of fucking Ginger Rogers," I said. Tony added, "Yeah, every now and then he gets to talking about her and he won't shut up". Then Kenneth said, "you would think every producer in Hollywood is after her the way Stan talks." "I've never heard him mention his sister", Donny said. "You want to have some fun" I asked. "Yeah," answered Donny. "When Stan comes in, just ask him how his sister is doing. I promise you, he'll start raving about her. We'll make a bet on how long he talks about her. I'll say one hour." Tony bet one hour and a half and Kenneth bet two hours. The trap was now set. In about 30 minutes, Stan walked in. We all grinned at Donny. Stan was going over some paperwork. Donny walked over to his desk and said, inquisitively, "How's your sister, the dancer, doing Stan?" Stan looked up and had a serious look on his face. "What are you talking about, Donny?" "Your sister, the dancer. I heard she was a great dancer." "Donny, you've got a warped sense of humor. For your information, my sister was in a car wreck when she was 16 years old and she's been in a wheelchair for the past ten years. I don't think you're funny a fucking bit." Then, Stan threw his paperwork on the desk, got up, and hurried out of the office. Needless to say, Donny's mouth was wide open and he had this "I just shit in my mess kit", look on his face. He ran after Stan. Stan got in his car and sped off. Donny came back in the office and said "You mother-fuckers ought to be ashamed." About this time, Stan slipped back in the door. He was laughing. We all started laughing. "We got you, didn't we?" "Yeah, you really did." Then he looked at Stan and said "I bet your sister really is a good dancer, Stan." "I'm sure she would be if I had one, but I don't have a sister." After that, Donny couldn't wait to pull the joke on the next unsuspecting victim.

I mentioned that my captain was Captain Marrow. Well, he was a big man of stature and had been with the police department for 15 years prior to my becoming an officer. We were sitting around his office one day telling "war stores" and he told about an ex-police officer named Wesley Tripp. Wesley left the police department in the 50's and went to work in construction. He was a slight built man but as Captain Marrow described "tough as nails". Wesley had a habit of drinking heavily on the weekends and invariably his wife would have to call the police to take Wesley to jail. It seems he would become violent and she feared for her life. Anyway, Captain Marrow explained that the inspector (same as captain) then, was Matthew Roman. I was familiar with Inspector Roman; he was on the force in 1961 when I became an officer. I remembered him as a huge guy with the biggest hands I had ever seen. He would shake your hand and it reminded you of your childhood days when you shook hands with your dad. Anyway on this particular night, Wesley had again started drinking. And, as usual, his wife called the police. The dispatcher put out the call and as she routinely did when Wesley was involved, sent two cars and the sergeant. You see, it normally took four or five officers to control

Wesley. When the call went out, Captain Marrow related that Inspector Roman came on the air and said; "Cancel those other cars. Just send the zone car. I'll back them up." The zone car arrived on the scene and shortly after, Inspector Roman pulled up. Captain Marrow said Inspector Roman got out of his car and told the officers who were standing at the foot of the front porch steps, "I'll show you guys how to handle this asshole." Then Inspector Roman walked up the steps and stood at the front door. This was an old frame house and there was a long banister on each side of the door way. Inspector Roman kicked the bottom of the door and said "Wesley, get your ass out here." Wesley opened the front door and said, "What the fuck do you want?" "Wesley, you're going to jail." Inspector Roman then reached for Wesley's left arm. Captain Marrow said that was a mistake. He said Wesley hit Inspector Roman right on the forehead. He said the punch actually picked Inspector Roman up off the porch and he went backwards over the banister and onto the ground. He landed beside the two officers; you guessed it, on his big ass. Captain Marrow said that the only thing Inspector Roman said was "Get that mother-fucker and lock him up." The officers called for back-up and once again, it took five officers to arrest Wesley. Inspector Roman did not participate in the arrest.

Toward the end of my days in vice, some of the tact squad officers were temporarily transferred to vice in order to attempt some drug buys. Most of the regular vice officers were known to the dealers. Some of the dealers, we found, had taken pictures of us when we appeared in court, so, we needed fresh blood. One such officer was Ronnie Halfacre. Ronnie was just an old country boy who loved to fish. He really wasn't very familiar with the drug world. We thought, however, that he might be able to buy some dope. We briefed him and sent him to the house of a known drug dealer. We told him the dealer went by the name of "Frog Man".

We drove to a location where we could observe the buy and secure the safety of Ronnie. So, here goes Ronnie, wearing his blue jeans, plaid shirt, tennis shoes and a hat with a fishing fly pinned to the front. Ronnie walked up to the front door and knocked. A female answered the door and looking suspiciously at Ronnie asked "what do you want?" "Is Frog Man here?" Ronnie asked. "No, he ain't" she replied harshly. Then Ronnie asked the conversation ending question, "Well, are you Mrs. Frog Man?" The woman slammed the door in Ronnie's face almost knocking him off the porch. We were bent over laughing and poor Ronnie walked over to us and said, "What did I do wrong, guys?"

Captain Marrow told another "war story" which involved an officer by the name of Mutt Hemmingway. This story took placed back in the 50's so there really weren't any repercussions from Officer Hemmingway's actions. Anyway, Captain Marrow and Mutt were working together as patrol officers and they received a call in one of the alleys in a low rent district. Upon arrival, they saw a man standing and holding his head which was covered with blood. They got out of their cruiser and by then, a crowd had gathered. The man was talking loud and explaining that someone had hit him in the head with a rock. Mutt told the man to calm down and asked him if the rock were still around. Captain, I mean Officer Marrow, was wondering why Mutt asked about the rock. It seemed apparent that the man had been hit with some very hard object. Anyway the man said, "Sure, that's the rock" as he pointed to a large rock on the ground near his feet. Mutt asked if anyone had touched the rock after he got hit and the man said "no". Marrow was thoroughly confused now but he didn't say anything. Mutt then pulled out his handkerchief and placed it over the rock. "We're gonna take the rock and have it dusted for fingerprints. If we can match them to a perpetrator, will you prosecute him?" "I sure will" replied the injured man.

Mutt told Marrow to get in the patrol car and he followed. He then told Marrow to drive to the end of the alley, turn around and drive back by the man. Marrow said, "Have you lost your mind, Mutt? Why did you tell that man we were gonna dust the rock for prints?" "Just do what I said, Marrow" answered Mutt. So, Marrow drove to the end of the alley, turned around and started towards the man who was standing there, still bleeding and relating the events of the evening to all. As the cruiser approached the man, Mutt leaned out the window of the patrol car and shoved the rock into the man's chest knocking him to the ground. Mutt then shouted, "You dumb mother-fucker, you can't get prints off a rock." Marrow, sensing a dire need to exit the scene, sped off. He said Mutt turned to him and calmly said, "Can you believe anyone is that stupid?"

Captain Marrow told me that once, he and Mutt were working together and they got a "fight call". Captain Marrow was driving and using his emergency lights and sirens. Just before they arrived at the scene, Mutt shouted "Stop the car, Marrow." Captain Marrow sensing that Mutt had seen something bad happening, stopped the cruiser in the middle of the street. He said Mutt got out of the care and got into a vehicle beside them. In that vehicle was a young lady and she and Mutt drove off. Captain Marrow was left there in the middle of traffic with siren blaring and lights flashing. He said when he went in for relief that night, his sergeant asked him where Mutt was and he told the sergeant that Mutt got sick and he took him home. He said Mutt didn't show up for work for over a week. When Captain Marrow inquired where he had been, Mutt said "I shacked up with that good looking gal." What made this story shocking, if you will, was that during the time Mutt was "missing", the Mayor made some promotions and, that's right, Mutt was picked to be promoted to sergeant. The problem was, nobody could find him, so the Mayor skipped over him and promoted someone else. When told this, Captain Marrow said that Mutt just shrugged his shoulders and said "Oh well, the stripes weren't worth giving up the pussy." As I said, this took place in the 50's.

Chapter VIII

Peaches, K-9s, the Nudist and Farm Animals

It is now 1975. Pet rocks and mood rings are popular fads. I have transferred back to the patrol division. This is where it all started and this is where I will finish my career as a police officer. I was assigned to the south sector. There were several female officers in the field now. One of the females I worked with was a short, oriental looking female who went by the nickname "Peaches". Peaches and I were working together one night when we received a break-in of a business in our zone. Upon arrival, we saw that a K-9 officer had already arrived and was waiting to put his dog in the building. There was a huge hole in the front door where someone had thrown a breeko block through it. Not knowing if anyone (burglar) was inside, the K-9 officer took his dog, which was a large, long-haired German Sheppard, inside the building. Peaches and I were standing on the sidewalk in front of the door where they entered. After a few minutes, we got a little lax. We shouldn't have. We were standing with our backs to the door when Peaches turned and said, "Oh shit". About the same time, I heard the toenails of the K-9 hitting the sidewalk. He had come to the front of the building and seeing us, decided to attack. Peaches headed for our car which was about 30 feet from where we were standing. She hit the front seat with me right behind her. When I hit the seat, I also hit Peaches. I said frantically, "Move over". She couldn't. She was wedged between the arm rest and me. Neither of us could move. The K-9 was closing in. I looked back and I could see the biggest set of K-9 teeth I had ever seen. My left leg was completely exposed outside the car. Feeling that the situation was hopeless, I just closed my eyes and tried to prepare for the imminent pain. Then, like a voice from above, I heard what turned out to be the most saving word I have ever heard, "Stop". It was Officer Bill Stevens, the K-9 officer. Almost as quickly as the danger began, it ended. The dog stopped in his tracks, turned and went to Bill. I reached down to check my leg and make sure it was still there. Peaches then started laughing. Somehow, I failed to see the humor then, but had I been in her position, I probably would have laughed, also.

Speaking of K-9s, there was an officer in our detail named Jim Boyd. Jim was a guy who always said clever thinking, kinda like Don Rickles. Once, Jim walked up to this real short attorney outside city court. Jim looked him over and said "You must handle small claims." Well, the attorney was furious. He reported Jim and the chief gave him an oral reprimand. Anyway, Jim bought this big Doberman. He put him in a fenced area of his backyard and decided he would train him to be an attack dog. One day after consuming a couple beers,

Jim headed out to the backyard. When he opened the gate and went inside, the Doberman attacked him and chewed him up pretty bad. Jim crawled out of the backyard and went back inside his house. He then went to his family doctor and the good doctor sewed him up. He gave Jim a tetanus shot and sent him home. On the way home, Jim stopped and got a six pack. He went home, and after consuming three or four more beers, headed back to the dog pen, this time more determined to train his Doberman. Guess what, Jim opened the gate, went inside the pen and the dog attached him again. The dog opened up several new wounds on Jim. Again, Jim crawled out of the dog pen and went inside his house. He went back to see his doctor again and after sewing Jim up again, the doctor told him, "Jim, you might consider getting you a Chihuahua."

Ever been in a situation where you wanted to laugh but couldn't because it just wouldn't be appropriate? This next incident describes such a time. Officer Bennie Foster and I were working together on nights when we received a 10-43 (investigation) talk to an officer call. The address was in an established neighborhood. The houses were well kept and probably 40 to 50 years old. Upon arrival, we were met at the front door by a lady in her late 70s. She escorted us to her den, or as she referred to it, her parlor. There, we were introduced to another lady who was also in her 70s. They asked that we be seated. We took a seat on the couch and the ladies sat in the chairs across from us.

The lady who resided there began the conversation by telling us that she had received a disturbing phone call that night. She said that she didn't know what we could do about the call but she felt that she should report it. She said, "Earlier tonight I answered the phone and a voice on the other ended sounded like a young man. He said hi, how are you doing? I said I'm fine. He talked for about a minute or so and then he said he wanted to ask me a question. I asked what that was and he said, I bet you have a good cock." I warned you that this was one of those situations where you wanted to laugh but couldn't. I knew better than to look at Officer Foster. So, I tried to think about everything that I could that was of a serious nature. I thought of murders, robberies and car wrecks – anything but what the lady had said. I tried to comfort the lady by telling her that it was more than likely a prank call and that the person would probably not call back. Then she said, "I'm not finished officer. He then repeated it." I was thinking please don't say it again, lady. But, she did; She said, "I'm sorry" and he said it again, "I bet you have a good cock." I could feel the vibration of Officer Foster's body shaking. He was about to lose it. I stood up abruptly and said, "Ma'am, this is what you need to do." I went through the suggestions that we offer anyone complaining about obscene calls. I figured the only way to keep from laughing was to do all the talking.

After doing this, I informed her that she need not show us to the door. We would find out way out. I just couldn't risk hearing her say "I bet you have a good cock" any more. Officer Foster and I left and from that day on, we had a greeting for each other. You got it – "I bet you have a good cock."

Normally, on the day shift you answer mostly boring calls, calls like burglary of a business, illegally parked cars, thefts, etc. Well, this call I received on the day shift was far from boring. I received a 10-43 (investigation) call at a residence which was located on a street that bordered the river. Seems a lady had uncovered (excuse the pun) a nudist camp next door to her own residence. When I arrived and knocked, I was greeted by a somewhat drab looking woman who appeared to be of a shy nature. She explained that the people next door to her were lying in the backyard with some friends and they were all naked. She directed me to a window in her kitchen and asked that I look out. The window was small and above my head and I could not see out. Since she was much shorter than me, it seemed impossible that she could see anyone naked next door. She then said, "here stand on this chair". I told her I would go next door and investigate her complaint but since they couldn't be seen from the street and the river was behind (again, excuse the pun) there probably wasn't anything I could do. Anyway, I left the complainant's house and went next door. As I approached, I observed five male and four females lying face down on towels. When one of the men saw me, he said "Hi officer, can I help you?" All of the sunbathers began moving and not knowing their intentions, I said, "Don't get up". I explained the situation to them and I left since I had not witnessed any violation of the law. As I got back into my squad car, I felt a sense of pride. I was always instructed that a good officer has to think fast and I felt I had done so. As I was driving off, I met three other squad cars who had headed to the call to "back me up". It told them that the show was over and noticed the disappointed looks on their faces. I wondered if any of them would have thought fast enough to have said "don't get up".

I told you about Peaches, the oriental looking female I worked with. Well, Peaches, like me, enjoyed contributing funny adlibs at roll call. One day, I was the victim of one of her adlibs. So, after the laughter died down, I looked at her real serious and said, "Peaches, I still haven't forgotten Pearl Harbor". Everyone laughed but Peaches.

I got one on one of my "little" partners after roll call one day. My partner was Gary Clinton, no relation to the President. Gary was a very short man, but as I often told him, he made up for that by being skinny. Anyway, the Mayor had come to our roll call on the day shift and made a plea for our support in the upcoming Mayor's race. After roll call, he was walking around and talking to the officers individually. As I mentioned, we were working the day shift and there weren't many officers at roll call. The Mayor walked over to Gary and me and said "You guys are kinda short today, aren't you?" I spoke up and said, "They're not all his size, Mr. Mayor. Some of the guys are tall." The Mayor, thinking Gary had been offended, apologized. I assured him that I was joking. Finally, thank goodness, he laughed.

I had a lot of fun with Gary and fortunately he had a sense of humor. One night, near Christmas, we went to the Waffle House to get some coffee. Contrary to public opinion, we never ate doughnuts. So, anyway we're in the Waffle House and I was seated. Gary walked over to the table where I was and before he knew what was happening, I grabbed him and sat him in my lap. I said out loud, "Now tell Santa what you want for Christmas, little boy."

Now let me tell you about an incident that happened on the midnight shift. I worked with a partner named Doug Livingston. Doug had this habit of sleeping when I was driving.

This usually occurred around 4 or 5 a.m. I didn't mind so much his sleeping, but he snored very loud and sometimes it was difficult to hear the police radio due to the loud vibrations of his snoring. We worked the lake area, so one morning I decided to break Doug from sleeping. As usual, about 4:30 Doug fell sound asleep. I drove to the lake area and backed the patrol car down one of the boat ramps. The water was up to the bottom of the front doors when I stopped. I roused Doug and said, "Doug, I'm gonna take a leak. You need to go?" He opened his eyes about half way and with saliva running down his chin, said "Yeah, I better go." Doug opened his door and stepped out into about a foot of lake water. "What the hell's going on?" I was cracking up, "You really had to go, didn't you Doug?" You know, after that morning Doug stayed awake every time we worked together. I told a few of the guys about my getting Doug; just a few.

It was breaking daylight one morning and Doug and I were in a park in our zone. We had parked beside a lake and had decided to "rest our eyes."

All of a sudden, there was a loud knocking on the door glass where Doug was resting. He jumped up into an upright position and, with his hair in a mess and drooling, saw a lady standing outside his door.

He said, "Yes, could I help you?" She responded that a car on the other side of the lake looked suspicious to her. Doug answered, "Yeah, we have them under surveillance." The lady asked how we could see them while in a reclining position. Doug replied, "We've got surveillance cameras on top of the patrol car and we can see them without being noticed."

What is amazing, in afterthought, is that she actually believed that. After we left, I asked Doug if he really thought she believed him and he said, "Sure, I thought I was very convincing." I reminded him that even though we might be unnoticed, I thought the marked police car would indicate our presence.

One of the officers related to me a story about how he had accomplished the same results with his partner. It seems that his partner would nap almost every time they worked the midnight shift (11 p.m. to 7 a.m.) He decided to try and break his partner. The officer who slept was Officer John Hudson. The officer who broke him was Officer Joe Stanton. Joe was a farm raised boy and he was knowledgeable about farm animals. On the shift in question, John, as usual, decided to catch a nap. He got in the back seat and stretched out. Joe and John worked the rural section of the city and Joe stopped on the outskirts of their zone. He pulled the car onto a field and stopped the engine. It was a warm night and John had rolled his back window down. Joe waited for the surprise. This field was occupied by several horses. After they had been parked there for about an hour, it happened. All of a sudden, John let out this blood curdling scream from the back. "Help, Joe, get it off me." It seems that one of the horses had walked up to the car and being curious, stuck its head inside the back window. You can imagine waking up and seeing a horse's head staring at you. The horse, hearing John's scream, pulled its head from the window and ran back to the other horses. Joe was rolling in the front seat. Joe later told me, "You know something? John never did sleep again when we were working together." "I wonder why," I asked.

Speaking of farm animals, I have to tell you the story that was contributed by one of the older officers. There was this single officer who was a farm bred guy and was in his late 60s. Well, some of the other officers decided to fix him up with this "lady". Seems the lady had an appreciation for police officers. The officers arranged for the older officer, John Strong, to meet the lady. After getting off one night, some of the officers got the lady and brought her to the rear of the station. They convinced Mr. Strong, as we all called him, to get in the car with the lady. Well without hesitation, Mr. Strong, got in the car and took care of business. After the lady left, one of the officers asked Mr. Strong, "You didn't kiss her did you?" "I sure did" he quickly replied. "Did you know that she gives head jobs?" "I don't care" answered Mr. Strong. "I'd kiss a mule if I was fucking it."

Now, let me tell you about something that happened after one of our softball games. The police department had an inter-departmental softball league. We played ball on the west side of town and one night after an invigorating game, that we had won, several of us went to one of the local drive-in markets to consume some beer. We were behind the market and had been there about 30 minutes when this young black male walked to the middle of the circle that we had formed. He pulled up one of his sleeves and displayed about 10 or 15 watches. "Any of you guys want to buy a nice watch, real cheap?" One of the officer-ballplayers walked up to the guy and said "You must be the unluckiest motherfucker in the city." "Why's that, man?" He inquired. "Because you just walked into the middle of a police officer softball team and tried to sell us some hot watches." "Oh no, man." "Oh yes" the officer said. We called the zone car and had the subject, along with his portable jewelry store, transported to headquarters.

Chapter IX

Rookies and the Sulphur Well

It's now the 80's. Designer jeans by Calvin Klein, Gloria Vanderbilt and others are the fashion craze. I take the physical, oral and written tests and become an MPO, master patrol officer. Along with my regular duties, my new duties will be to work with rookies after their graduation from the police academy. We have three sectors – the east, west and south sectors. We have come a long way from the small building where it all started for me in 1961. The rookies will spend two months at each of the three sectors, where they will be instructed and evaluated at the end of each two month period.

Now I would have my chance to get the new guys like the older guys got me when I was a rookie. Don't get me wrong. What we did was 90% work and 10% play. I choose to use those figures, anyway. The first day a rookie got into the car with me, I would let him or her know that they were there to learn. I would inform them that they would be doing the things that I would normally do. The rookies only worked the night and morning shifts. No day shifts. One of our duties on the morning shift was to check the business section of our zone for break-ins. I had this one service station where the owner kept two ferocious dogs in his building at night. So, while on patrol, I would pull up to the service station and I would say something like "That door doesn't look right, how about checking it?" The rookie would, of course, get out and walk to the door. As soon as he turned the knob, the two dogs, a Doberman and German Sheppard, would come out of nowhere and attempt to attack the rookie through the door. It would scare the hell out of the rookie. I would then say something like, "Oh, I forgot to tell you about the dogs."

Another thing I got a kick out of was the rookies' reaction when I used my double talk on them. Being anxious to do well, as all rookies should be, they were very interested in the orders from the field sergeant. So, when it was quiet and we were driving around the zone, I would say something like, "The sergeant said to be sure to check all the ferbers tonight." The rookie would respond, "Check the what?" "I said the sergeant said to check all the ferbers in the cosbin." "I still don't know what you said." "Well, if you're not gonna listen, just forget it." The rookie, not wanting to offend me, would just sit there with this puzzled look. Then, during the shift, if we happened to signal 8 (meet) another zone car, which was occupied by another rookie, my rookie would always get the other rookie to the side and I knew he was asking about the ferbers. The other rookie, of course, had no idea what he was talking about.

One thing I did with the rookies, especially the females, was to drive by this certain area of the zone that sometimes had a foul smell. If the smell were noticeable, I would explain that there was a sulphur well on the property at one time. Then, if I had intestinal gas, which I often had on the morning shift, I would drive by that area and "cut the cheese". I would then ask "Do you smell that sulphur?" The rookie would reply, "I sure do and it smells awful." Yeah, I would say they ought to do something about that.

The last joke I'll mention that I inflicted on the rookies was my "sleepy joke". When you're on the morning shift, usually around 4 or 5 a.m., it gets quiet. The police radio has less transmissions and the traffic gets lighter. There used to be an old saying that during the early morning hours, the only people on the streets were cab drivers, thieves and police officers. Anyway, when it got real quiet, I would be driving and I would cease the conversation between the rookie and me. I would then shut my right eye, giving the impression that I was going to sleep. I would keep my left eye on the road and let the patrol car drift to the right shoulder of the road. The rookie would, in a panic, grab my arm and shake it in an attempt to wake me. I would ask "What's the matter with you?" "You were going to sleep," the rookie would reply. "No I wasn't" I would respond. The rookie, not wanting to offend me, would usually apologize. I would do this three or four times before the rookie would suggest "Want to get some coffee?" After having the coffee, the rookie would request my letting him drive. To end the stress for the rookie, I would say, "Okay, just be careful."

    Each time I pulled a joke on the rookie, my thoughts went back to that night on the switchboard. Those immortal words from Lieutenant Morris, "We're getting 'em young and stupid". I hope you can see me now lieutenant, I've come a long way.

Chapter X

Saying Goodbye

Receiving my 25 year pin

It is now 1986. Nancy Reagan launches "Just Say No" anti-drug campaign and I just say no to my police career. It's over and exactly 25 years to the day, I retire. The last day ended as it started 25 years ago with a moment of humor. I was working the day shift and just before relief time, I received this call, "Headquarters to 33." "Go ahead, 33". "We have a report of a loose bear. The owner states the bear is tame but needs our assistance in locating him." "Did you say, as in Smokey Bear?" "10-4, 33." I started towards the area and I was thinking, the last day I work and they still haven't quit pulling jokes on me. In about ten minutes, the oncoming detail began to check in. "Headquarters to 33." "Go ahead, 33." "Signal 9 (disregard) the bear has been located." "10-4, 33." I headed for the south station. I would have to turn in my paperwork and my car for the last time. I was having very mixed emotions. On one hand, I was glad to be retiring. Some of my fellow officers were not so fortunate. They had given the supreme sacrifice. They didn't make it to retirement.

"Car 313 to 33." It was one of the detective cars calling me. "Go ahead." "Signal 12." Signal 12 was the code for switching to another frequency where you could converse with another officer. "10-4, 33." "Car 313 to 33, this is Summers Bobby. Good luck. I heard it was your last day. We're gonna miss you". "Thanks Summers. I'll miss all you guys too." While I was on the other frequency, cars started calling me from all over the city. Each officer was telling me good-bye. Now, the tears were starting to flow. Stop, I thought. Police officers are supposed to be tough. Then, one of the female dispatchers, a black lady named Miss Eaton, came on the air. "We're gonna miss you Bobby. You're one of the best."

When I got to the south station, my lieutenant met me and told me that he needed to see me in the assembly room one last time. When I opened the door, my entire detail, even some who were off duty that day, were inside. The room was decorated and refreshments were in abundance. My detail presented me with an Airweight 38 revolver. They had it engraved. It ready, Bobby Bass 1961 to 1986. I thanked them all and said "I love you all." And I do.

Made in the USA
Charleston, SC
10 July 2010